Affirmations
of Faith, Purpose and Intention

Treiva Williams

© 2024 Treiva Williams All rights reserved. No part of this publication may be reproduced, distributed, or transmitted in any form or by any means, including photocopying, recording, or other electronic or mechanical methods, without the prior written permission of the publisher, except in the case of brief quotations embodied in critical reviews and certain other noncommercial uses permitted by copyright law. ISBN 979-8-35097-577-2

Hi there!

First and foremost; thank you; your choice to read, share and actively engage with this book is appreciated and affirms me personally in ways you will never understand.

I want to personally welcome you on this journey with "Affirmations of Faith, Purpose, and Intention." This book isn't just about reading affirmations; it's about letting these affirmations resonate deeply within you, hopefully transforming not only your mindset but the very essence of your daily life.

The heart of this book lies in the belief that words, when truly embraced, have the power to change and shape our reality. It's about moving beyond merely reciting affirmations to letting them infuse our actions, decisions, and interactions with faith, purpose, and intention. This is a journey of hope—a promise that the words you declare can and will manifest into tangible changes in your life.

Accompanying each affirmation are self-action promises and daily accountability assignments. These are crafted to ensure that the vibrancy of each affirmation doesn't fade away but is actively applied to your life. It's about making a personal commitment to live out the truths declared in these affirmations, to see them as actionable beliefs rather than fleeting thoughts and mere words. Whether it's learning to see challenges as opportunities for growth, or finding joy in everyday moments, these promises to yourself and assignments of accountability guide you to take meaningful steps towards living a life aligned with your deepest values and dreams.

Declaring each affirmation with faith, purpose, and intention is like opening a door to a world where your dreams and reality converge. It's about nurturing hope within you—a hope that believes in the beauty of your dreams and your power to achieve them. My little book is my personal invitation to you to not just hope for a brighter, more fulfilling life but to actively create it, one affirmation at a time.

My sincere hope and prayer is that as you go through the pages of this book, you approach each affirmation with an open heart and a hopeful spirit. I pray you allow these words to take root in your life, guiding you towards a future brimming with possibilities.

The potentially most impactful pages of this book beyond the affirming declarations of faith purpose and intention are the blank pages that are there to allow you to reflectively affirm in your own words with honesty and vulnerability the thoughts and reflections that each declaration brings forth for you.

This journey is not just about envisioning the life we desire but about stepping into it with grace, courage, and a hopeful heart.

So again, welcome to this hopeful journey. Declare each affirmation with faith, purpose and intention; in full expectation of manifested results within yourself.

I'm believing all of God's best for you!

Treiva

SELF-CONFIDENCE

Building self-confidence has been more of an inner journey than I ever expected. It's about more than just pumping yourself up for big moments or presenting a polished exterior. For me, it's rooted in the quiet affirmations I tell myself on days when things don't go as planned or when doubts start to creep in. It's about acknowledging my strengths and accomplishments without a but or a maybe tacked on the end.

This growing self-confidence shapes how I face the world. It's like putting on a pair of glasses that helps me see my potential clearly, not distorted by the lens of insecurity or fear. It's learning to trust my instincts and embrace my unique qualities, quirks and all. There's real power in simply standing firm in who you are, in not just hearing but really listening to that inner voice that says, "You've got this." With each small victory, whether it's speaking up in a meeting or tackling a project I used to think was beyond me, that voice gets louder. Self-confidence doesn't mean I'm devoid of doubts, but it does mean I'm getting better at not letting those doubts rule me. It's about celebrating the small steps just as much as the leaps, knowing that each one is a testament to growing a bit more into the person I aspire to be.

I DECLARE WITH FAITH, PURPOSE & INTENTION
I am capable of achieving my dreams.

Self-Action Promises:
1. Clearly define my dreams and write them down.
2. Create a step-by-step plan to achieve these dreams.
3. Take one small action today towards these goals.

Accountability Assignment:

Identify one significant dream and map out a detailed action plan for the next month.

"I pray the strength within me will illuminate the path to my dreams. Let each step I take be guided by determination and creativity. Give me the courage to allow myself to be open to opportunities and ready to overcome obstacles, moving steadily towards my aspirations. AMEN!"

I DECLARE WITH FAITH, PURPOSE & INTENTION

Confidence in who I am, whose I am & who I'm striving to become grows stronger every day.

Self -Action Promises:

1. Start each day with positive affirmations about my strengths.
2. Set and achieve small, daily goals to build confidence.
3. Reflect on successes at the end of the day.

Accountability Assignment:

Keep a daily journal or progress tracker for one week, noting each success and how it felt.

"With each new day, may my confidence be solidified. I embrace my strengths and accept my weaknesses, understanding that both contribute to my unique self-authenticity. May I radiate self-assurance and inspire others through my journey. AMEN!"

I DECLARE WITH FAITH, PURPOSE & INTENTION
I trust in my abilities to succeed.

Self -Action Promises:
1. Identify my core strengths and skills.
2. Seek opportunities to apply and enhance these skills.
3. Seek feedback to understand and improve abilities.

Accountability Assignment:

Choose one skill to improve and practice it consistently for the next two weeks.

"As I move towards success, I trust in the abilities You have graced me with. May this trust be the foundation of my actions and decisions. As I face challenges, let my trust in You & myself be unwavering, guiding me towards my goals. AMEN"

I DECLARE WITH
FAITH, PURPOSE & INTENTION
I am worthy of all the good in my life.

Self-Action Promises:
1. Practice gratitude by acknowledging good things in my life daily.
2. Surround yourself with positive influences.
3. Engage in acts of self-care and kindness towards myself.

Accountability Assignment:
Write a letter to yourself, expressing why you are deserving of all the good in your life.

"May I always recognize and cherish the goodness that surrounds me. Let me always be mindful and believe that I am deserving of happiness, love, and success. Let me embrace these gifts from You with gratitude, sharing my joy with others. AMEN"

I DECLARE WITH FAITH, PURPOSE & INTENTION
Every challenge I face makes me stronger.

Self-Action Promises:
1. View challenges as learning opportunities.
2. Develop a strategy to approach and overcome obstacles.
3. Reflect on past challenges and the strengths gained.

Accountability Assignment:
Identify a recent challenge and analyze how it has made you stronger. Write down the insights and lessons learned.

"God help me to remember that each challenge I face is an opportunity to grow stronger. I pray that resilience be my ally, and that every difficulty lay way to the refinement and fortification of my spirit. I declare I will emerge stronger and more capable in spite and because of my adversity. AMEN!"

GRATITUDE

Gratitude has woven itself into the fabric of my everyday life, subtly transforming my perspective in ways I didn't see coming. It's not just about those big, banner moments of success or joy; gratitude really shows its power in the quieter instances. Like feeling thankful for that first sip of coffee in the morning or appreciating a text from a friend just checking in. It's these small pulses of gratitude that build up over time, creating a steady rhythm of appreciation in my daily life.

The more I've made gratitude a habit, the more I've noticed how it shifts my focus from what's lacking to what's overflowing. There's a kind of magic in recognizing the abundance around you, even in simplicity. It could be as mundane as being grateful for the bus arriving on time or the smooth functioning of your old laptop. Every time I acknowledge these little blessings, I feel a bit lighter, a bit more grounded. It's like gratitude isn't just an emotion; it's a lens that colors my interactions and choices, making the ordinary sparkle with the extraordinary. By regularly counting my blessings, I'm not just tallying up good things—I'm training my mind to spot joy and potential in every corner of life. It's an ongoing journey, but one that enriches each step with a profound sense of contentment and presence.

I DECLARE WITH FAITH, PURPOSE & INTENTION

I am grateful for every experience that shapes me.

Self-Action Promises:
1. Keep a journal of challenging experiences and the lessons learned from them.
2. Practice acknowledging both positive and negative experiences as part of growth.
3. Share stories of experiences and their impacts with a trusted friend or family member.

Accountability Assignment:
Reflect on a significant experience and write about how it contributed to your personal growth.

"God, I pray that I recognize and embrace every experience as a valuable lesson. Let gratitude be my guide, as each event shapes me into a stronger, wiser person. In joy and in challenges, I am thankful for the growth they bring. AMEN!"

I DECLARE WITH FAITH, PURPOSE & INTENTION

My life is full of blessings and I appreciate each one.

Self -Action Promises:

1. Make a daily list of three blessings in my life, varying them each day
2. Express gratitude directly to people who have been a blessing to me
3. Practice mindfulness to be present and appreciate the blessings around me.

Accountability Assignment:

Spend a week capturing photos of daily blessings and create a gratitude collage.

"God, I recognize and am so grateful to be surrounded by blessings. Help me to always see and appreciate these gifts, big and small, understanding their value in my life's journey. AMEN.

I DECLARE WITH FAITH, PURPOSE & INTENTION
Gratitude fills my heart and guides my actions.

Self-Action Promises:
1. Begin each day by writing down what I am grateful for.
2. Perform a random act of kindness daily as a way to express gratitude.
3. Verbally express gratitude to at least one person each day.

Accountability Assignment:
Keep a gratitude journal for a week, noting how gratitude influenced your actions each day.

"God may gratitude continuously fill my heart, guiding my actions and interactions. May this sense of thankfulness for all that You provide for me through Your love, grace and mercy inspire kindness, generosity, and positivity in my daily life, influencing not just my actions but also those around me. AMEN"

I DECLARE WITH FAITH, PURPOSE & INTENTION
I find joy and beauty in the simplest things.

Self-Action Promises:

1. Take a daily walk, observing and appreciating the simple beauty around me.
2. Practice being fully present in everyday moments, finding joy in them.
3. Create something simple yet beautiful, like a drawing or a poem.

Accountability Assignment:

Spend an hour in nature, focusing on appreciating its simple beauty, and journal your experience.

"Thank You God that my eyes are open to the joy and beauty in the simplest aspects of life. Please let me continue to find happiness and appreciation in small moments and to count those blessings even in the valley moments of my life. AMEN!"

I DECLARE WITH FAITH, PURPOSE & INTENTION
Thankfulness brings peace to my mind.

Self-Action Promises:

Meditate for a few minutes each day, focusing on feelings of thankfulness.

1. Write down things I am thankful for when I feel stressed or anxious.
2. Practice deep breathing while thinking of things to be grateful for.

Accountability Assignment:

Create a 'thankfulness' jar, filling it with notes of gratitude each day for a month.

"God in moments of turmoil, may thankfulness be my anchor, bringing peace to my mind. As I remind myself of the many blessings in my life despite the momentary temporary presence of trouble, let tranquility overtake me, calming my thoughts and soothing my spirit. AMEN"

PERSEVERANCE

Perseverance has become this quiet companion that walks with me every day, nudging me to keep going even when the end isn't in sight. It's been less about heroic moments of triumph and more about the quiet resolve to keep pushing, even when things are downright tough. Sometimes, it's as simple as getting up five minutes earlier to squeeze in a morning stretch, or as tough as grinding through a project that feels like it's going nowhere. It's that gritty, behind-the-scenes work that nobody claps for, but boy, does it build something solid inside you.

Reflecting on this journey of sticking with it, I've realized that perseverance is about gathering little victories along the way. It's appreciating that even slow progress is progress. And you know what? There's something incredibly rewarding about looking back and seeing just how many mountains you've climbed, one small step at a time. It's not just about reaching that big goal but about growing stronger and more resilient with each little challenge that comes your way. Perseverance has taught me that the sweetest victories are often won in silence, and they're about more than success—they're about becoming the kind of person who doesn't back down when life gets real. It's like discovering a new depth to your spirit, one that whispers, "Keep going, you've got this," even when the odds seem stacked against you.

I DECLARE WITH FAITH, PURPOSE & INTENTION
I overcome challenges with courage and resilience.

Self-Action Promises:
1. Think back on a recent challenge and figure out a brave way to handle it.
2. Create a personal motto for staying resilient when things get tough.
3. Practice activities that help me stay strong and resilient.

Accountability Assignment:
Write about a challenge you've faced and how you dealt with it using courage and resilience.

"Let me face every challenge head-on with courage and not give in. I want to be strong in tough times, using these moments to push me forward. I'm ready to show how resilient I can be, turning every hard situation into a win. AMEN"

I DECLARE WITH FAITH, PURPOSE & INTENTION
Every setback is a setup for a comeback.

Self-Action Promises:
1. Reflect on a recent setback and look for the lessons in it.
2. Create a plan to turn my recent setback into a positive experience.
3. Talk to someone I admire about bouncing back from tough times.

Accountability Assignment:
Create a comeback plan for a recent setback, listing out steps for turning it around.

"God, In each setback, let me find the start of my next success. I want to see these hard times as chances to grow and come back stronger. Each challenge is just preparing me for something great ahead. AMEN"

I DECLARE WITH FAITH, PURPOSE & INTENTION
I persist until I succeed.

Self-Action Promises:
1. Pick a goal that's challenging but achievable and commit to it.
2. Track my progress and adjust my approach if needed.
3. Get inspiration from stories of people who never gave up.

Accountability Assignment:

Choose a goal you've put aside and make a new plan to achieve it.

"God, grant me the discipline and focus to stick with my goals until I make them happen. Even when it's tough, I won't give up. Every step I take, no matter how small, is moving me towards my dreams. AMEN!"

I DECLARE WITH
FAITH, PURPOSE & INTENTION
My determination is stronger than any obstacle.

Self-Action Promises:
1. Think about what motivates me and keep that in mind.
2. Break a big challenge into smaller steps I can manage.
3. Celebrate every small success on my way to overcoming this challenge.

Accountability Assignment:

Write a plan for getting over a current challenge, detailing each step and your determined approach.

"May my determination be unshakeable, no matter what I face. When I come across obstacles, I want them to make me even more determined. Whenever I doubt myself, I'll remember just how capable I am of overcoming anything. AMEN!"

I DECLARE WITH FAITH, PURPOSE & INTENTION
I learn and grow from every difficulty.

Self-Action Promises:
1. Reflect on a recent difficulty and write down what I learned from it.
2. Apply a lesson from a past challenge to my current situation.
3. Share what I've learned with others, helping them too.

Accountability Assignment:

Keep a 'growth journal' for a month, tracking how each challenge contributes to your personal growth.

"With each difficult moment, I hope to learn something new and grow stronger. I want to view challenges as lessons that make me wiser and more resilient. I know and accept every hard time is a chance for me to evolve and be my best self. AMEN!"

MINDFULNESS

 Embracing mindfulness has been like tuning into a frequency that I didn't even realize existed before. It's about slowing down in a world that constantly rushes forward, about finding stillness when everything around screams chaos. Mindfulness isn't just a practice; it's a way of experiencing life moment to moment, breath by breath. It's taught me to notice the subtle flavors in my morning coffee, the soft texture of the light at sunrise, and the calm in a deep breath taken during a stressful day.

 This journey into mindfulness has shifted how I interact with the world and myself. It's less about controlling my environment and more about observing it, engaging with it softly without judgment. By being present, I've discovered how to listen more deeply—not only to others but to my own inner dialogues. The chatter in my mind isn't as loud these days; there's more room for peace, more space for understanding. And in those quiet spaces, I find small joys and insights that might have slipped by unnoticed. Mindfulness reminds me that every day is stitched together with moments that deserve attention and appreciation. Each time I manage to stay present, even if just for a few minutes, I feel like I'm right where I'm supposed to be, fully alive and connected.

I DECLARE WITH
FAITH, PURPOSE & INTENTION
I am fully present in every moment.

Self-Action Promises:
1. Practice mindful breathing for a few minutes each day to anchor myself in the present.
2. Focus on one task at a time to avoid multitasking.
3. Actively listen during conversations, fully focusing on the speaker.

Accountability Assignment:
Spend the day practicing mindfulness; write down or note moments when your mind wanders and gently bring it back to the present.

"God I pray to be deeply present in my now, embracing each moment with full awareness and appreciation. Let me soak in the beauty and intricacies of the here and now, cherishing every experience as it unfolds. God may my mind be free from the distractions of the past, concern and worry of the future, allowing me to live fully and vibrantly in every second, appreciating life's fleeting moments. AMEN!"

I DECLARE WITH
FAITH, PURPOSE & INTENTION
Peace resides within me at all times.

Self-Action Promises:

1. Find a quiet spot each day to sit quietly and connect with my inner peace.
2. Use positive affirmations to remind myself of the peace within.
3. Avoid situations and discussions that disrupt my inner tranquility.

Accountability Assignment:

Create a peaceful corner in your home where you can sit and meditate or reflect peacefully for a few minutes each day.

"God, I thank you that within me lies a sanctuary of peace, constant and steadfast because of Your presence, grace and mercy. Help me to connect with this peace that only You can give during life's storms, finding solace and strength in its depths. Let this inner peace be the calm in my heart, guiding me through tumultuous times and serving as a source of comfort and resolution. In my moments of unease and insecurity, may I remember the reservoir of peace that dwells within, accessible and enduring. AMEN!"

I DECLARE WITH FAITH, PURPOSE & INTENTION
I embrace the present with an open heart.

Self-Action Promises:
1. Start my day by setting an intention to remain open to all experiences.
2. Consciously let go of past regrets and future worries periodically throughout the day.
3. Engage in activities that require me to be present, like art or gardening.

Accountability Assignment:

Create a journal entry at the end of the day about how you stayed open to today's experiences and what you learned from them.

"God, I welcome every present moment with an open heart, ready to receive all that it has to offer me. Thank you for the joy I find in learning, and in right now opportunities, free from the weight of what was or what might be. As I go through each day, let me be receptive to the myriad of experiences, embracing them with warmth and eagerness. In this openness, may I discover the richness of life, fully engaging with the world around me. AMEN!"

I DECLARE WITH FAITH, PURPOSE & INTENTION:
Each breath I take is an opportunity for peace.

Self-Action Promises:
1. Practice deep breathing exercises for a few minutes each day.
2. Use moments of stress as cues to focus on my breath.
3. Integrate short breathing breaks into my daily routine.

Accountability Assignment:

For one week, begin and end your day with a five-minute deep breathing session, focusing on the peace it brings.

"God with each breath I take, may I draw in peace and calm, and with every breath I release with it goes the tension and worry I'm carrying. Let this continuous cycle of breathing be a reminder of the ever-present opportunity for peace within me. In moments of stress or discomfort, may my focus on breath bring me back to a state of calm, reminding me of the power I hold to cultivate peace at any moment AMEN"

I DECLARE WITH FAITH, PURPOSE & INTENTION:
I am aware and appreciative of the beauty of the now.

Self-Action Promises:

1. I'll make time for a daily walk, taking in and appreciating my surroundings.
2. I'll maintain a gratitude journal, noting the every-day beauties I come across.
3. I'll consciously reduce distractions like frequent phone use to stay more present.

Accountability Assignment:

Today, capture photos of things simple yet captivating and build a collection of today's wonders.

"God, allow me to truly see and appreciate the beauty in every moment. May I find joy in both the simple and the magnificent, discovering the many wonders my life has to offer right now. With a clear and grateful heart, I aim to notice the world's beauty as I move through my day, staying mindful and fully engaged with life as it unfolds around me. AMEN"

GROWTH AND PERSONAL DEVELOPMENT

Growth and personal development have become my quiet, constant companions on this winding journey called life. It's not about monumental changes overnight or transforming into someone entirely new. Instead, it's about those little tweaks, small decisions, and subtle shifts that accumulate over time. Like choosing to read a bit more instead of scrolling through my phone, or deciding to speak up in situations where I'd usually stay quiet. Each choice feels like a tiny sculpting tool, gradually shaping the person I'm becoming.

This path of personal development is filled with self-discovery and sometimes, self-doubt. But that's part of the growth, isn't it? Learning to lean into discomfort, to embrace the unknown as an opportunity rather than a threat. It's fascinating to look back and see not just how much I've changed, but how much more aligned I feel with my values and dreams. The real joy of personal growth isn't just in achieving goals or acquiring skills—it's in the blossoming of self-awareness and the expanding horizon of my potential. Every day presents a new chance to learn something, to improve, to grow—and that's incredibly empowering. It turns every challenge into a teacher and every setback into a stepping stone. I'm learning to celebrate progress, no matter how small, and to trust the process, embracing each day as another stroke on the canvas of my life.

I DECLARE WITH FAITH, PURPOSE & INTENTION:
Every day, I evolve into a better version of myself.

Self-Action Promises:
1. Set small daily personal development goals.
2. Reflect on personal growth at the end of each day.
3. Adopt a new positive habit monthly.

Accountability Assignment:

Write down one specific thing you did better today compared to yesterday.

"God, today I acknowledge and thank You for my growth, no matter how small, and celebrate the steps I take in self-improvement. May I be kind to myself in this journey, recognizing that growth is a continuous process filled with learning, adapting, and evolving. With each experience, may I gain insight and wisdom, as I move closer to the person I aspire to be. AMEN"

I DECLARE WITH FAITH, PURPOSE & INTENTION:
I embrace new experiences as opportunities for growth.

Self-Action Promises

1. Say ‹yes› to a new opportunity each week.
2. Learn a new skill or hobby.
3. Engage with people from diverse backgrounds.

Accountability Assignment:

Identify and write down one new experience today and describe how it did or can contribute to your growth.

"God today I welcome new experiences with an open heart and mind, seeing them as rich opportunities for personal growth and betterment. Grant me the courage to step into the unknown, embracing challenges and adventure. I pray these experiences broaden my understanding, enhance my skills, and enrich my life, causing me to grow in ways I never imagined; for this God I am thankful. AMEN!"

**I DECLARE WITH
FAITH, PURPOSE & INTENTION:
I recognize earning and growing is
a continuous journey for me.**

Self-Action Promises:

1. Dedicate time for learning daily.
2. Attend workshops or seminars.
3. Engage in intellectual discussions.

Accountability Assignment:

Spend 30 minutes today learning something new and journal about it. Try to incorporate this at least weekly going forward.

"God, as I go through life and face each new day may I not be so consumed by my desired destination that I forget or take for granted the journey and the opportunities/experiences along the way. As I walk through life, may I cherish the ongoing journey of learning and growing. Let my mind be open to new ideas, my heart receptive to new experiences, and my spirit eager for continuous self-enhancement. May my path to a better me and life be a lifelong journey of learning and enrichment to my life, keeping me curious, adaptable, and always ready to grow. AMEN!"

I DECLARE WITH FAITH, PURPOSE & INTENTION:
Mistakes are steppingstones to my success.

Self-Action Promises:
1. Reflect on mistakes to learn from them.
2. Share and discuss errors for collective learning.
3. Maintain a 'lessons learned' journal.

Accountability Assignment:
Reflect on any mistakes of the day, write them down, and identify the lesson or positive outcome.

"God because I trust and believe that ALL things ultimately work for my old may I view each mistake as an essential step towards my success. Let my mistakes and mishaps never be in vain and cause me to learn and recognize valuable lessons from every error, using these insights to build a wiser, stronger path forward. In each mistake, may I find resilience and determination, transforming challenges into opportunities for growth and achievement. AMEN!"

I DECLARE WITH FAITH, PURPOSE & INTENTION
I am committed to personal excellence.

Self-Action Promises:
1. Set a challenging goal for today
2. Seek constructive feedback regularly.
3. At the end of the day celebrate your achievement.

Accountability Assignment:
Set and accomplish a small, specific goal for today aligned with personal excellence, and reflect on the progress at the end of the day.

"God, in my pursuit of personal excellence, may my commitment be unwavering and my efforts consistent. Let me set high standards for myself, striving to achieve them with dedication and integrity. In this journey towards excellence, may I find satisfaction in my hard work and pride in my achievements, continuously seeking to improve and excel in all aspects of my life. AMEN!"

POSITIVITY AND OPTIMISM

Positivity and optimism have become my guiding stars, transforming the way I navigate through life's ups and downs. It's not about wearing rose-colored glasses or ignoring the challenges that come my way. Instead, it's about choosing to see the potential for good in each situation, about holding onto the belief that things can improve even when the odds seem stacked against me. This perspective isn't just hopeful thinking; it's a deliberate choice to focus on the silver linings, making it a bit easier to weather the storms.

Embracing this positive outlook has taught me resilience in a profoundly personal way. Each time I encounter setbacks, I try to ask myself, "What can I learn from this?" rather than spiraling into despair. Optimism doesn't remove obstacles, but it does provide a light to see them more clearly and find ways around them. It's about laughing more, worrying less, and trusting in my journey, knowing that even the detours are leading somewhere worthwhile. This approach has opened up a world of possibilities, where challenges are just invitations for innovation, and failures are merely steppingstones to success. Living with a positive mindset enriches every day, making life not just bearable, but vibrant and full of hope.

I DECLARE WITH
FAITH, PURPOSE & INTENTION
I choose to see the good in every situation.

Self-Action Promises:
1. Actively look for a positive aspect in difficult situations.
2. Practice gratitude daily, acknowledging the good around me.
3. Encourage others to find the positive in their own challenges.

Accountability Assignment:
Write down one challenging situation you encountered and the positive aspect you found in it.

"In every circumstance, may I find the strength to focus on the good. Let me approach each situation with a mindset that seeks positivity, finding silver linings even in challenging times. May this perspective bring light to my path and hope to my heart, fostering resilience and joy within me. AMEN!"

I DECLARE WITH FAITH, PURPOSE & INTENTION
Positive thoughts shape my wonderful reality.

Self-Action Promises:
1. Replace negative thoughts with positive affirmations.
2. Visualize positive outcomes for my goals.
3. Surround myself with positive influences and environments.

Accountability Assignment:

Reflect on your thoughts throughout the day and write down how you redirected negative thoughts into positive ones.

"May my thoughts be a garden where positivity blossoms, shaping a reality that is bright and wonderful. Let me nurture optimistic thoughts, allowing them to guide my actions and influence my life's journey. In this mindset, may I find happiness, fulfillment, and peace. AMEN!"

I DECLARE WITH
FAITH, PURPOSE & INTENTION
I radiate positivity wherever I go.

Self-Action Promises:
1. Greet people with a smile and positive words.
2. Offer help or support to someone in need.
3. Share a positive message or story with others.

Accountability Assignment:
Note down how you spread positivity to at least one person during your day.

"As I move through my day, may I be a beacon of positivity, radiating hope and joy in every interaction. Let my presence bring comfort and positivity to others, creating an atmosphere of optimism and kindness wherever I go. AMEN!"

I DECLARE WITH FAITH, PURPOSE & INTENTION
Optimism is my natural state of mind.
Self-Action Promises:

1. Begin each day with a positive affirmation.
2. Look for the good in every situation, especially in difficulties.
3. Maintain a hopeful outlook on future possibilities.

Accountability Assignment:

Write down three things that went well during your day and how your optimistic mindset contributed.

"In the ebb and flow of life, may optimism be my anchor, my natural state of mind. Let this optimistic outlook infuse my thoughts and actions, helping me to face life's challenges with hope and positivity. In this state, may I inspire others and find joy in the simple pleasures of life. AMEN!"

I DECLARE WITH
FAITH, PURPOSE & INTENTION
I will find reasons to smile every day.

Self-Action Promises:
1. Find humor in everyday situations.
2. appreciate the small joys and achievements of each day.
3. Share a smile or a kind word with others.

Accountability Assignment:
At the end of the day, write down what made you smile and how it affected your mood and those around you.

"Each day, may I discover countless reasons to smile. Let joy be found in the small moments, the simple pleasures, and the beauty of life. In this practice, may I spread happiness to those around me, sharing the gift of a smile. AMEN"

HEALTH AND WELL-BEING

Health and well-being have become more than just routine check-ups and hitting the gym; they're about nurturing a harmony between my mind, body, and spirit. It's been a shift from viewing health as a series of stats—like calories burned or steps taken—to understanding it as a holistic balance. This perspective turns every decision about food, sleep, or exercise into a meaningful choice rather than a compulsory task. Each meal, each night's rest, or each walk becomes an act of self-respect.

This journey into deeper health awareness has been enlightening. It's taught me to listen—really listen—to what my body tells me. Those little aches or moments of fatigue? They're not just nuisances but messages, cues to take it easier or mix things up. As I've aligned more with my body's needs, I've noticed how much my mood and energy levels have improved. Mental clarity and emotional stability often seem just as nourishing as a well-balanced meal. Embracing well-being in this comprehensive way has made me realize that true health is less about pursuing an ideal and more about finding my unique rhythm and balance. It's a continuous, rewarding journey that enhances how vividly I experience each day and how resiliently I bounce back from setbacks.

I DECLARE WITH FAITH, PURPOSE & INTENTION:
My body is healthy; my mind is brilliant; my soul is tranquil.

Self-Action Promises:
1. Engage in physical activity daily to maintain bodily health.
2. Dedicate time to activities that stimulate the mind and enhance knowledge.
3. Practice mindfulness or meditation to cultivate inner peace.

Accountability Assignment:
Note down physical, mental, and spiritual activities of the day and how they contributed to overall well-being.

"May each body be a temple of health, each mind a sanctuary of brilliance, and each soul a haven of tranquility. Let these elements work in harmony, creating a balance of physical wellness, mental sharpness, and inner peace for all. In this state of holistic health, strength to pursue goals and calmness to enjoy life's journey is found. AMEN!"

I DECLARE WITH FAITH, PURPOSE & INTENTION
Every cell in my body vibrates with energy and health.

Self-Action Promises:
1. Eat nutritious foods that energize and heal the body.
2. Stay hydrated and mindful of the body's hydration needs.
3. Ensure adequate rest and sleep for cellular regeneration.

Accountability Assignment:
Track food, water intake, and sleep quality, noting their contributions to energy levels.

"God, may every cell in my body be charged with vitality and health, infusing strength and endurance. Allow my spirit, body, emotions and mentality tackle every day with enthusiasm and a zest for life. AMEN!"

I DECLARE WITH FAITH, PURPOSE & INTENTION:
I nourish my body with healthy choices.

Self-Action Promises:
1. Choose whole, unprocessed foods as often as possible.
2. Listen to the body's hunger and fullness signals.
3. Plan meals to include a variety of nutrients.

Accountability Assignment: Record meals and snacks, reflecting on how they nourish and support the body.

"God, may my choices made each day nourish and strengthen my body. Help me to be mindful of the foods consumed, choosing those that offer vitality and health. In this practice of nourishment, may my body be well-equipped for life's adventures. AMEN!"

I DECLARE WITH FAITH, PURPOSE & INTENTION:
MY Mental and physical well-being is my priority.

Self-Action Promises:

1. Schedule regular physical exercises and mental relaxation activities.
2. Set aside time for hobbies and interests that relax and invigorate.
3. Regularly assess and adjust lifestyle to support well-being.

Accountability Assignment:

Note down physical and mental wellness activities and their impacts.

"Let well-being be at the forefront of priorities. Cherish both mental and physical health, dedicating time and effort to maintain and enhance them. In this balance of mind and body, find the strength and clarity for a fulfilling and prosperous life. AMEN!"

I DECLARE WITH FAITH, PURPOSE & INTENTION
I am grateful for my health and vitality.

Self-Action Promises:
1. Practice gratitude daily, acknowledging the body's capabilities and strengths.
2. Share the journey of health and vitality to inspire others.
3. Respect the body's needs and treat it with kindness and care.

Daily Accountability Assignment:
Write down three aspects of health and vitality to be grateful for each day.

" God it is with gratitude, I acknowledge the gift of health and vitality in my physical, mental and emotional being. I pray this thankfulness reminds me to cherish and care for myself every day. AMEN!"

SUCCESS AND ACHIEVEMENT

Success and achievement have taken on new meanings in my life; they're no longer just about reaching the top of a ladder or ticking off goals. Instead, they've become markers of personal fulfillment and progress. It's about setting my own standards and celebrating the milestones that truly resonate with my values and aspirations. Whether it's mastering a new skill, improving a relationship, or completing a challenging project, each achievement is a testament to my journey and growth.

This evolution in understanding success has encouraged me to embrace each step of my endeavors, not just the outcome. It's recognizing that the path to achievement is often zigzagged, filled with learning and unexpected turns rather than a straight sprint to the finish line. By shifting my focus from end results to the richness of the process, I've found greater satisfaction and motivation. Each small success builds my confidence and spurs me onward, reminding me that achievement isn't just about the accolades or applause but about the personal satisfaction of knowing I gave it my all. This mindset turns every effort into a victory, no matter the scale, enriching my life with a sense of true accomplishment and continual aspiration.

I DECLARE WITH FAITH, PURPOSE & INTENTION
I am on the path to great achievements.

Self-Action Promises:
1. Set clear and achievable goals towards great achievements.
2. Stay committed to daily tasks that lead to these goals.
3. Regularly review and adjust the path to ensure alignment with aspirations.

Accountability Assignment:

Each evening, reflect on and note down the steps I took that day towards a significant goal.

"God I thank You that I am on a journey towards great achievements. I pray my determination and perseverance be strong as I turn my aspirations into realities. God, let each step I take be filled with wisdom and courage, paving my way to remarkable accomplishments. AMEN!"

I DECLARE WITH FAITH, PURPOSE & INTENTION
Success is attracted to my positive energy.

Self-Action Promises:
1. Cultivate a positive mindset and outlook each day.
2. Surround myself with positive influences and people.
3. Use affirmations to reinforce my positive energy and success.

Accountability Assignment:

Write down moments where my positive attitude influenced or attracted a successful outcome.

"God I pray my positive energy I put forth attract success in all my endeavors. I will nurture optimism and a positive outlook, drawing opportunities and accomplishments towards me. God in this aura of positivity and hopefulness, I aim to reach my goals and realize my dreams. AMEN!"

I DECLARE WITH
FAITH, PURPOSE & INTENTION
I celebrate every small victory on my journey.

Self-Action Promises:
1. Recognize and appreciate small accomplishments daily.
2. Share my achievements with friends or family to magnify the celebration.
3. Keep a journal of all my victories, big and small.

Accountability Assignment:
At the end of the day, write down at least one small victory and reflect on its significance.

"God as I travel on my journey I promise with purpose. and intention to celebrate every small victory. I will acknowledge and cherish these triumphs, seeing them as vital milestones. God, I recognize in celebrating these moments, I find motivation and joy, fueling my journey towards greater successes. AMEN!!"

I DECLARE WITH FAITH, PURPOSE & INTENTION
My actions create constant prosperity.

Self-Action Promises:

1. Take consistent and deliberate actions towards my personal and professional growth.
2. Make informed and strategic decisions that foster prosperity.
3. Continuously seek opportunities for improvement and advancement.

Accountability Assignment:

Track my daily actions that contribute to personal and professional prosperity.

"God, I pray my actions lead to a constant flow of prosperity. May each decision and effort I make contribute to my journey of success and abundance. In this path of action, I aim to reap a bountiful harvest of achievements, reflecting my hard work and dedication as provided to me through your grace and mercy. AMEN!!"

I DECLARE WITH FAITH, PURPOSE & INTENTION
I am deserving of my dreams and achievements.

Self-Action Promises:
1. Affirm my worth and deservingness of achievements daily.
2. Set goals that reflect my aspirations and work diligently towards them.
3. Celebrate my personal strengths and progress regularly.

Accountability Assignment:
Write down how today's efforts and qualities reinforced my deservingness of dreams and achievements.

"God, because of You I firmly believe in my worthiness and deservingness of my dreams and achievements. Through hard work, talent, and dedication, I affirm this deservingness. May my confidence grow, paving the way for me to realize my dreams and celebrate my achievements. AMEN!"

LOVE AND RELATIONSHIPS

Navigating the realms of love and relationships has become a profound and enriching part of my life's journey. It's less about finding the perfect someone and more about cultivating meaningful connections that resonate deeply and authentically. This exploration into the dynamics of relationships has taught me the value of understanding, patience, and genuine communication. Each relationship, whether fleeting or lasting, is a chapter in the story of my emotional growth, teaching me more about myself and how I relate to others.

Embracing love in all its forms—romantic, platonic, familial—has shown me that the essence of strong relationships is not in mere harmony but in how we navigate the disagreements and challenges. It's in these moments that the depth of a bond is tested and often strengthened. By fostering a spirit of openness and empathy, I've found that relationships become not just a source of comfort but also a platform for mutual growth and inspiration. This approach has transformed my interactions, turning them into opportunities for deeper connection and understanding, making every heartfelt conversation and shared laughter a building block for lasting bonds. Love, I've realized, is not just about giving or receiving but about sharing and growing together, creating a tapestry of experiences that enriches every aspect of life.

I DECLARE WITH FAITH, PURPOSE & INTENTION
I am surrounded by love in all forms.

Self-Action Promises:

1. Acknowledge and appreciate the different forms of love encountered daily.
2. Create an environment that fosters love and kindness.
3. Share love through acts of kindness and compassion.

Accountability Assignment:

Note down the moments of love experienced throughout the day, whether in nature, interactions, or thoughts.

"God, help me recognize that I am enveloped in love in its many forms. May I see your presence in the gentle morning breeze, the warmth of a friend's smile, and in every aspect of my life. Guide me to cherish these manifestations of love each day. Amen."

I DECLARE WITH FAITH, PURPOSE & INTENTION
Every relationship in my life is meaningful and fulfilling.

Self-Action Promises:
1. Nurture relationships by investing time and genuine interest.
2. Communicate openly and with empathy to deepen connections.
3. Celebrate the uniqueness of each relationship.

Accountability Assignment:
Reflect on a relationship and identify what makes it meaningful and fulfilling.

"God, I thank you for blessing me with relationships that bring meaning and fulfillment. Help me to cherish the unique contribution of every individual and to foster connections that are rich in understanding, support, and joy. Amen."

I DECLARE WITH FAITH, PURPOSE & INTENTION
I attract positive and loving people into my life.

Self-Action Promises:
1. Radiate positivity and kindness in interactions.
2. Seek out and engage in communities that value positivity and love.
3. Be open to forming new relationships with positive individuals.

Accountability Assignment:
Identify a new or existing connection that brought positivity into the day.

"God, guide me to be a beacon for positive and loving people. Let my energy resonate with kindness and warmth, drawing similar spirits into my life for mutual support and positivity. Amen."

I DECLARE WITH FAITH, PURPOSE & INTENTION
Love guides all my relationships.

Self-Action Promises:
1. Approach relationships with a loving and open heart.
2. Use understanding and empathy in all interactions.
3. Cultivate an atmosphere where love is the foundational principle.

Accountability Assignment:
Reflect on how love guided interactions and decisions in relationships today.

"God, let love be the guiding force in all my relationships. Foster within me understanding, patience, and a deep connection, creating bonds that are strong and nurturing. Amen."

I DECLARE WITH FAITH, PURPOSE & INTENTION
I express love and respect with all my interactions.

Self-Action Promises:
1. Show love and respect in both words and actions.
2. Practice active listening and empathy in conversations.
3. Treat each interaction as an opportunity to spread kindness and respect.

Accountability Assignment:
At the end of the day, evaluate how love and respect were expressed in interactions.

"God, in every interaction, help me to express love and respect. May these values shine through in my words, actions, and gestures, creating positive and respectful exchanges with everyone I encounter. Amen."

COURAGE AND FEARLESSNESS

Embracing courage and fearlessness in my life has been like stepping into a clearer, more vibrant version of the world. It's not about the absence of fear, but rather the decision to stand up and face it head-on. This journey of cultivating bravery has revealed that the moments I decide to push beyond my comfort zones are the very ones that define and expand the boundaries of my life. Whether it's speaking my mind in a crowded room, tackling a new project, or even reaching out to mend a strained relationship, each act of courage confirms that fear is not a roadblock but a gateway to new experiences.

This exploration into fearlessness has taught me that courage isn't a grand, one-time spectacle; it's a series of small, everyday choices. It's choosing to rise each morning with the intention to make the day slightly better than yesterday, despite the uncertainties that lie ahead. Every time I choose action over hesitation, I chip away at the walls of fear that seek to confine my spirit. And in doing so, I've discovered that courage breeds more courage, setting off a ripple effect that not only empowers me but also inspires those around me. It's about finding the strength to be vulnerable, to open up, and to connect genuinely—knowing well that the essence of fearlessness lies in the will to keep moving forward, even when the path isn't clear. This approach transforms not just how I view challenges but how I live each day, turning life into a thrilling adventure that's lived fully and fearlessly.

I DECLARE WITH FAITH, PURPOSE & INTENTION
I face challenges with bravery and confidence.

Self-Action Promises:
1. Approach challenges head-on with a positive mindset.
2. Cultivate self-confidence through preparation and practice.
3. Embrace new challenges as opportunities to grow.

Accountability Assignment:
Identify a challenge faced today and reflect on how it was approached with bravery and confidence.

"God, grant me the strength to face challenges with bravery and confidence. Let me confront each obstacle with a courageous heart, secure in the knowledge that I am capable and strong. Amen."

I DECLARE WITH
FAITH, PURPOSE & INTENTION
Fear is just a feeling; I overcome it and move forward.

Self-Action Promises:
1. Acknowledge fears without letting them control actions.
2. Practice positive self-talk to counteract fearful thoughts.
3. Take small, deliberate steps to overcome fears.

Accountability Assignment:
Write down any fears encountered today and how they were overcome.

"God, remind me that fear is merely a feeling, not a fact. Help me to overcome it and move forward with determination and courage. In your guidance, I find the strength to push past my fears. Amen."

I DECLARE WITH FAITH, PURPOSE & INTENTION
I am unstoppable in the pursuit of my dreams.

Self-Action Promises:
1. Stay focused and committed to personal goals.
2. Persist through challenges and setbacks.
3. Maintain a clear vision of the end goal.

Accountability Assignment:
Note down progress made towards a dream or goal today.

"God, instill in me an unstoppable spirit in the pursuit of my dreams. Let no obstacle deter me, and let my determination be unwavering. With your support, I am relentless in the pursuit of my aspirations. Amen."

I DECLARE WITH FAITH, PURPOSE & INTENTION
My courage inspires others.

Self-Action Promises:

1. Lead by example, showing courage in all endeavors.
2. Offer support and encouragement to those facing their own challenges.
3. Share personal stories of courage to motivate others.

Accountability Assignment:

Reflect on an instance where courage was displayed today and how it might have inspired others.

"Dear God, let my courage be a source of inspiration to others. May my actions demonstrate strength and bravery, encouraging those around me to embrace their own courage. Together, we can face life's challenges. Amen."

I DECLARE WITH FAITH, PURPOSE & INTENTION
I am fearless in the face of any adversity.

Self-Action Promises:
1. Tackle adversities head-on with a steadfast spirit.
2. Build resilience through facing and overcoming challenges.
3. Stay calm and composed in the face of adversity.

Accountability Assignment:
At the end of the day, reflect on any adversities faced and how they were handled fearlessly.

"God, in the face of adversity, endow me with a fearless heart. Let me confront each challenge with unwavering courage, secure in the belief that I can overcome any obstacle. Amen."

BALANCE AND HARMONY

Balance and harmony—two ideals that often seem elusive yet essential. For a long time, I thought balance meant having everything in my life perfectly organized, with equal attention given to every responsibility. But over time, I've come to realize that true balance isn't about rigidly distributing my time and energy; it's about embracing the natural flow of life. Harmony, for me, is understanding that different areas of my life will require more attention at certain moments, while others may take a backseat temporarily—and that's perfectly fine.

In the pursuit of balance, there's a tendency to feel guilt when we're not giving equal energy to every part of our lives. But I've learned that balance isn't about maintaining perfection; it's about staying in tune with what's truly needed at any given time. Some days, work demands my full focus, and other days, my family or personal well-being needs to come first. It's not about neglecting one for the other, but about finding peace in the ebb and flow, trusting that everything will align in its own time.

Living in harmony means releasing the pressure to have everything under control at once. It's about being fully present where I am, honoring the different seasons of life, and knowing when to step forward and when to step back. There's a freedom in letting go of the need to juggle everything perfectly, in accepting that life will naturally shift and sway.

I've come to appreciate that balance is not a fixed state, but rather an ongoing process—an evolving journey. Some seasons will demand more action and drive, while others will call for rest and reflection. In learning to listen to what each moment requires; I find a deeper sense of peace. It's in this gentle rhythm of giving and receiving, doing and being, that true harmony is found. And in that space, life becomes not a constant struggle to keep everything equal, but a beautiful dance of intention and grace.

I DECLARE WITH FAITH, PURPOSE & INTENTION
I live my life in balance and harmony.

Self-Action Promises:
1. Prioritize tasks to ensure a balanced lifestyle.
2. Regularly assess and adjust life areas to maintain harmony.
3. Integrate relaxation and mindfulness into daily routines.

Accountability Assignment:
Reflect on the day's activities to ensure they contributed to a balanced and harmonious life.

"God, lead me on a path where balance and harmony are at the core of my existence. Help me to intertwine the many aspects of my life – work, family, self-care – into a beautiful tapestry of equilibrium. May I find peace in balance, ensuring that no part of my life overwhelms the others, and live each day in a harmonious blend of productivity and relaxation. Amen."

I DECLARE WITH
FAITH, PURPOSE & INTENTION
I find peace and joy in both work and play.

Self-Action Promises:
1. Find joy and fulfillment in professional tasks.
2. Make time for leisure and activities that bring happiness.
3. Seek a healthy balance between work and personal life.

Daily Accountability Assignment:
Identify moments of peace and joy in both work and play today.

"God, bless me with the ability to find peace and joy in all facets of my life. In my professional endeavors, grant me fulfillment and satisfaction; in my leisure, let me find relaxation and happiness. May I approach both work and play with an open heart, discovering the unique joys each brings. Help me to blend these elements seamlessly, creating a life filled with contentment and bliss. Amen."

I DECLARE WITH FAITH, PURPOSE & INTENTION
My mind, body, and spirit are in perfect harmony.

Self-Action Promises:
1. Engage in activities that nourish the mind, body, and spirit.
2. Practice mindfulness to synchronize mental and emotional well-being.
3. Regularly participate in physical activity and spiritual practices.

Accountability Assignment:
Reflect on how daily activities contributed to the harmony of mind, body, and spirit.

"God, I seek harmony in my mind, body, and spirit. May these elements of my being work together in perfect unison, creating a symphony of well-being and inner peace. Help me to nourish each aspect equally, understanding that they are interconnected and essential for my overall health. In this state of harmony, let me find the strength to pursue my goals and the serenity to embrace life's beauty. Amen."

I DECLARE WITH
FAITH, PURPOSE & INTENTION
I maintain balance in all areas of my life.

Self-Action Promises:
1. Allocate time and resources evenly across all life areas.
2. Regularly evaluate and adjust commitments to avoid overextending.
3. Practice saying 'no' to maintain a healthy balance.

Accountability Assignment:

Assess how today's choices contributed to balance across different areas of life.

"God, help me to maintain a harmonious balance in every aspect of my life. From my professional responsibilities to my personal relationships, my health, and my spiritual growth, let each area receive the attention and care it deserves. Guide me to make choices that promote equilibrium, preventing any one area from overshadowing the others. In this balance, let me find the true essence of a fulfilling and content life. Amen."

I DECLARE WITH FAITH, PURPOSE & INTENTION
Harmony surrounds me at all times.

Self-Action Promises:
1. Create and maintain a peaceful and harmonious environment.
2. Approach conflicts and challenges with a mind-set focused on harmony.
3. Cultivate relationships that promote mutual respect and understanding.

Accountability Assignment:
Note any moments of discord and reflect on how they were resolved to restore harmony.

"God, surround me with an aura of harmony wherever I go. In my home, my workplace, and in my interactions, let there be a prevailing sense of peace and balance. Help me to be a source of harmony for others, radiating calmness and understanding in all situations. In moments of potential conflict, grant me the wisdom to seek resolutions that restore harmony and strengthen bonds. Amen."

CREATIVITY AND INNOVATION

Creativity and innovation have morphed into the heartbeats of my everyday existence, transforming mundane tasks into explorations of possibility. It's less about groundbreaking inventions and more about viewing the ordinary through a lens of curiosity. Whether it's tweaking a recipe, rearranging my living space, or brainstorming a new approach at work, each act of creativity fuels my spirit and pushes the boundaries of my imagination.

This journey of embracing creative thinking has taught me that innovation isn't confined to artists or inventors; it's accessible to anyone who dares to ask, "What if?" and "Why not?" It's about breaking the mold of routine thinking and allowing fresh ideas to surface, even in the smallest of tasks. As I've woven creativity into the fabric of my daily life, I've noticed a significant shift in how I solve problems and overcome challenges. Thinking outside the box has become a habit, one that leads to unexpected solutions and opportunities. Embracing this mindset has not only made life more interesting but has also fostered a sense of freedom and excitement. It's invigorating to know that with a little creativity, I can turn even the most basic project into something extraordinary, proving time and again that the magic really does happen outside the comfort zone.

I DECLARE WITH FAITH, PURPOSE & INTENTION
My imagination is boundless and creative.

Self-Action Promises:
1. Cultivate curiosity and openness to new experiences.
2. Dedicate time to creative pursuits and hobbies.
3. Surround oneself with inspiring and diverse sources of creativity.

Accountability Assignment:
Each day, jot down a new idea or creative thought that came to mind.

"God, bless me with a boundless and creative imagination. Let my thoughts soar without limits, exploring new realms of possibilities and ideas. May my mind be a fertile ground for innovative concepts and visionary dreams. Guide me to use this gift to enrich not only my life but also the lives of those around me. Amen."

I DECLARE WITH FAITH, PURPOSE & INTENTION
I find creative solutions to my challenges.

Self-Action Promises:
1. Approach problems with an open and innovative mindset.
2. Explore multiple solutions and perspectives before making decisions.
3. Use brainstorming and creative thinking techniques to tackle challenges.

Accountability Assignment:

Reflect on a challenge faced today and the creative solutions or approaches considered.

"God, in the face of challenges, bestow upon me the ability to find creative solutions. Let me approach problems with a mindset that sees beyond the conventional, discovering innovative paths and solutions. May this creativity turn obstacles into opportunities for growth and learning. Amen."

I DECLARE WITH
FAITH, PURPOSE & INTENTION
Creativity flows through me with ease

Self-Action Promises:
1. Create a conducive environment for creativity to flourish.
2. Practice regular mental exercises to keep the creative juices flowing.
3. Embrace spontaneous inspiration and act on creative impulses.

Accountability Assignment:

Identify a moment where creativity flowed naturally today and document the experience or outcome.

"God, let creativity flow through me with ease and grace. May my ideas and expressions come forth naturally, enriching my projects and endeavors. Help me to maintain a state of flow where creativity is as natural as breathing. In this creative state, let me produce work that is both fulfilling and impactful. Amen."

I DECLARE WITH FAITH, PURPOSE & INTENTION

Each day, I express my creativity in new ways.

Self-Action Promises:

1. Experiment with different forms of creative expression.
2. Challenge oneself to step outside of the creative comfort zone.
3. Share creative work with others for feedback and inspiration.

Accountability Assignment:

Engage in a new creative activity or approach and record the process and insights gained.

"God, inspire me to express my creativity in new and exciting ways each day. Let me find joy in experimenting with different mediums and ideas, expanding my creative horizons. May these daily expressions of creativity bring color and innovation to my life and those around me. Amen."

I DECLARE WITH FAITH, PURPOSE & INTENTION
I am an innovator; my ideas are powerful and transformative

Self-Action Promises:
1. Continuously seek knowledge and inspiration to fuel innovative ideas.
2. Collaborate with others to refine and expand upon new concepts.
3. Take actionable steps to bring transformative ideas into reality.

Accountability Assignment:

Record an innovative idea developed today and plan steps to explore or implement it.

"God, as an innovator, let my ideas be powerful and transformative. Grant me the vision to see beyond the present and the courage to bring these ideas to life. May my innovations inspire change and progress, positively impacting the world. Amen."